# DAVID ATHERTON'S
# CHRISTMAS COOKBOOK
## for kids

## David Atherton

illustrated by
## Katie Cottle

### CANDLEWICK PRESS

I love the festive period and spending it with my rock, support, and beloved Nik (also Rey and Kai, too). I couldn't have written this book without my family.

DA

For Mum. Thanks for all the dinners (Christmas and otherwise).

KC

First US edition 2024

Library of Congress Catalog Card Number pending
ISBN 978-1-5362-3439-8

24 25 26 27 28 29 CCP 10 9 8 7 6 5 4 3 2 1

Printed in Shenzhen, Guangdong, China

This book was typeset in Alice and Mrs Ant.
The illustrations were created digitally.

Candlewick Press
99 Dover Street
Somerville, Massachusetts 02144

www.candlewick.com

All recipes are for informational and/or entertainment purposes only; please check all ingredients carefully if you have any allergies, and, if in doubt, consult a health professional. Adult supervision is required for all recipes.

## Introduction

At Christmas, it's important to let our family and friends know how much we love them. In a season of giving and sharing, what better way to show them that you care than with a homemade gift? So step into the kitchen and get ready to create beautiful bakes and magical memories to treasure forever.

In this book, you'll discover recipes to make delicious gifts and stocking fillers, perfect party food, and showstopper cakes to share during your Christmas celebrations. Whether you want to impress your friends with an amazing gingerbread house, eat your way through a chocolate Christmas pudding, or make a bang with a cake shaped like a Christmas cracker, this book has everything budding bakers need to get ahead for the festive season.

On a cold winter's day, there's nothing I enjoy more than playing Christmas music and dancing around the kitchen while I'm baking festive treats. And you can create your own special traditions too! Choose a Christmassy recipe from this book, tie on your apron, and have fun spending time together!

David

# Contents

## Christmas Cakes and Cookies

## Festive Showstoppers

# Holiday Pantry

Christmas can be a busy time of year! But if you buy your ingredients in advance and read each recipe carefully, then you can focus on having fun in the kitchen. Here are a few handy tips, tricks, and facts to help you.

 **Yeast** needs the right conditions to start growing. In this book we use fast-acting yeast. You can use fresh yeast, but you'll need to double the weight. Always make sure your yeast isn't expired.

 **Nuts** are eaten a lot at Christmastime. Not only are nuts tasty, but they are also healthy and add a lovely crunchy texture. There are lots of different nuts, and it's easy to switch them in a recipe. Try as many different varieties as you can.

 **Dried fruits** add sweetness to a bake, but they're also full of vitamins, minerals, and fiber, which are good for us. Dried fruits are eaten at Christmastime because it's harder to get fresh fruits in the winter.

 **Spices** are used a lot in Christmas bakes, especially cinnamon, ginger, and cloves. If you have lots of different spices in your kitchen cupboard, you can experiment and find your favorite flavor combinations.

 **Food coloring** is a great way to make a bake special at Christmas. I recommend using color gels or pastes as they don't change the consistency of your mixture. Look for natural food colors that are made from vegetables and fruits. Make sure you have enough red and green as these are the most Christmassy colors.

 **Root vegetables** like carrots, parsnips, and sweet potatoes make bread and cakes soft and, most importantly, healthier. Root vegetables are easy to find in winter—so perfect for Christmas recipes.

 **Butter and spreads** are used in a lot of cakes, pastries, and cookies. Some bakes are known for their buttery flavor, but there are lots of alternatives made with sunflower oil, soybeans, or vegetable oil.

 **Milks and yogurts** were traditionally made with cow's milk. Nowadays, you can buy all kinds of milks and yogurts made from plants, such as oat milk or soy yogurt.

If you have food allergies, or are cooking for someone who does, you need to check the ingredients list carefully.

## Weighing and measuring

- All recipes are measured in ounces (oz) and cups.
- tsp = teaspoon
- tbsp = tablespoon
- The oven temperatures are in degrees Fahrenheit (°F).

# Great Gifts

These gift-wrapping ideas add another touch of thoughtfulness to your homemade treats. And, best of all, you can reuse and upcycle leftover everyday items you find in your home.

## Make a gift box

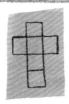

**1** Take a large piece of thin cardboard and draw a cross shape made up of 4 × 4 inch squares. The cross should be 4 squares high and 3 squares wide.

**2** Next, draw tabs (¼ inch high) on the top and bottom edges of the side panels and the bottom edge of the bottom panel.

**3** Cut around the outside edges and then use a ruler to help you fold and unfold along all the inside lines.

**4** Draw a fun Christmas design on one side.

**5** Turn it over and fold in all the tabs. Then fold in the panels closest to the side tabs and glue them in place.

**6** You should now have a box with a lid that is not stuck down.

**7** Place your baked gift or sweets inside the box and close the lid.

## Decorative jam jars

Make your special Christmas jam (p. 2) even more special by covering the metal lid with brown paper or leftover Christmas wrapping paper and tightly fastening with string or ribbon. Personalize it by writing and drawing on the top.

## Tied sandwich bags

Show off your sweet-and-spicy popcorn (p. 14) in a clear sandwich bag, perfect for sharing. Scoop in a few handfuls and secure with a bow!

## Gift-wrapped tubes

Give your leftover cookie or chip container another life! Decorate it with Christmas wrapping paper and fill it with a sweet surprise like the coconut snowballs (p. 4), then add a ribbon or bow.

# Equipment List

Before you begin, it's a good idea to check what equipment you might need. Here is a list of the basic equipment you will use in this book, but check each recipe individually too.

parchment paper

cake pans

baking sheets

cookie cutters

round cake pans

safety knife

cooling rack

cupcake tin

digital scale

festive plates and bowls for serving

mini foil baking cups

food processor

kitchen scissors

large mixing bowl

measuring cup

measuring spoons

muffin tin

oven mitts

oven timer

pastry brush

piping bags and nozzles

rolling pin

saucepan

sieve

spatula

cupcake liners

immersion blender

tea towel

whisk

wooden spoon

Remember to always ask an adult to help when you're baking. And don't forget to wash and dry your hands!

# Sweets and Edible Gifts

## Ingredients

5 cups frozen raspberries

½ cup granulated sugar

1 tsp allspice

1 tsp lemon juice

¼ cup chia seeds

### Makes 4 jars of jam

# Special Christmas Jam

This recipe is *really* special because it has raspberries—my favorite fruit for jam—and a touch of allspice and lemon to make it even more flavorful. Chia seeds get very sticky when wet, which is perfect for jam. I think the best way to eat it is on oatmeal, but you'll find lots of recipes in this book where you can use this jam.

**Top tip:** You can try making this jam with all sorts of fruit, like strawberries, cherries, or even blueberries.

## Method

**1** Add the raspberries, sugar, and allspice to a small saucepan.

**2** Ask an adult to help as you bring the ingredients to a simmer. Let the jam bubble away for 3 minutes, stirring continuously to help break down the fruit.

**3** Carefully take the pan off the heat, then stir in the lemon juice and chia seeds and leave to cool.

**4** When the jam has completely cooled, carefully pour it into 4 jars.

**5** Tie some ribbon around the jar and add a little gift label with a festive message on it.

**6** Give the jam to a friend as a gift and let them know to keep it in the fridge and use within 2 weeks.

# Crunchy Peanut Butter Cups

My husband is named Nik and these nutty treats are his favorite sweets. I make them for his birthday as well as Christmas. Using mini foil baking cups makes them extra special, but you can prepare this recipe in an 8-inch square cake pan and cut it into squares too.

## Ingredients

3 shortbread cookies
   (about 3 oz) or 3 graham
   cracker sheets
8 oz dark chocolate
¼ cup creamy peanut butter
About 60 roasted peanuts

### Makes 20 peanut butter cups

**Top tip:** You can use almond butter instead of peanut butter and top with almonds.

## Method

**1** Place 20 mini foil baking cups on a large baking sheet. (Or, if using an 8-inch square cake pan, line the pan with foil to keep the mixture from sticking.)

**2** Put the shortbread cookies in a sandwich bag and bash with a rolling pin until crushed into rough breadcrumbs, then empty into a mixing bowl.

**3** Break the chocolate into pieces and add to a small microwavable bowl. Ask an adult to help you microwave it for 30 seconds, then stir and repeat until it is melted and smooth.

**4** Add the peanut butter to the crushed cookies and mix until combined. Warm the peanut butter in the microwave for 20 seconds if it is too hard.

**5** Put a teaspoonful of melted chocolate into a cup, then add a teaspoonful of the cookie mixture. Top with another teaspoonful of melted chocolate and 3 peanuts.

**6** Repeat step 5 until you have used all the mixture. Refrigerate for at least 30 minutes, or until set.

# Coconut Snowballs

Truffles are fun to make, but the process does get a bit messy. I love it because you can lick your hands afterward and they taste really chocolatey (make sure you wait until the end, though). Adults love truffles, so maybe this is a good present to make for your parents or caregivers, as long as they like chocolate.

## Ingredients

4 oz dark chocolate

½ cup soft pitted dates

½ cup coconut milk

¼ cup coconut flakes

Makes 20 truffles

**Top tip:** Roll the truffles in all kinds of coatings like cocoa powder, crushed cookies, freeze-dried fruit, chopped nuts, or even sprinkles.

## Method

**1** Break the chocolate into pieces and add to a deep bowl, then set aside.

**2** Using scissors, cut the dates into chunks, removing any pits, then add the date pieces to a small saucepan.

**3** Pour in the coconut milk, then bring to a simmer over a medium heat for 3 minutes.

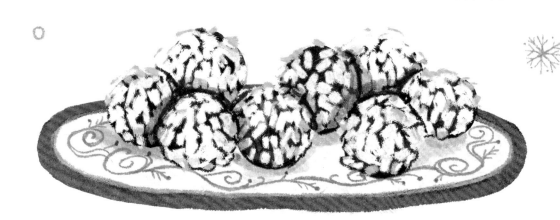

**4** Pour the mixture of dates and coconut milk over the chocolate, leave for 1 minute, then blend with an immersion blender until smooth.

**5** Cover and chill in the fridge for at least 3 hours.

**6** Just before you take the mixture out of the fridge, put the coconut flakes in a small bowl.

**7** This is the messy part! Scoop a small teaspoonful of the truffle mixture into your hands and quickly roll it into a ball shape (you have to be quick to keep the chocolate from melting too much).

**8** Roll the little ball in the coconut, then transfer to a plate and repeat with the remaining mixture.

**9** The truffles are best stored in the fridge and eaten within 3 days.

## Ingredients

1 lime

²⁄₃ cup unsalted butter
   (at room temperature)

1 tsp vanilla extract

½ cup granulated sugar
   (plus 2 tbsp for topping)

2 cups all-purpose flour

Green food color gel

1 medium egg white

1 cup powdered sugar

**Makes 30 small cookies (or 20 larger cookies)**

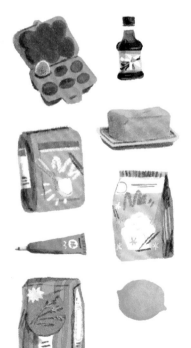

# Shortbread Trees

Shortbread is a buttery, crumbly cookie that is perfect for giving as a present as it tastes delicious and keeps nicely. For this recipe, we use royal icing, which sets really hard and gives the shortbread an extra crunch. You will need a small tree-shaped cutter, but if you don't have one, just use a different-shaped cutter, like a star or a circle shape for an ornament, and decorate with different colored icing.

## Method

**1** Line 2 large baking sheets with parchment paper.

**2** Ask an adult to help you carefully zest the lime using a fine grater into a large mixing bowl.

**3** Beat together the butter, vanilla extract, and ½ cup of sugar, then beat until creamy and smooth.

**4** Add the flour, then use your hands to mix everything together until it forms a stiff dough (if crumbly, add a little water).

**5** On a lightly floured surface, roll out the dough until it is ¼ inch thick.

**6** Cut out the dough with your tree-shaped cutter and place the trees on the baking sheets.

**7** Once you've used all the dough, chill the sheets in the fridge for 30 minutes.

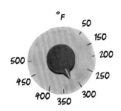

**8** Preheat oven to 325°F.

**9** Take the sheets out of the fridge, then bake for 12–15 minutes until golden brown at the edges.

**10** For the topping, add the 2 tablespoons of sugar and the green food coloring to a sandwich bag and shake so that the sugar turns green.

**11** Mix together the egg white and powdered sugar until you have a smooth, runny icing.

**12** Once the cookies are baked and cooled, dip them face down into the icing, then sprinkle with the green sugar. It takes a few hours for royal icing to set really hard.

**Top tip:** Add orange, lemon, or grapefruit zest if you like your shortbread extra zesty!

## Ingredients

12 sliced almonds

12 raisins

6 dried cranberries

6 mini pretzels

16 oz dark chocolate

3 ½ oz white chocolate

Makes 1 slab of bark

# Reindeer Chocolate Bark

Who wouldn't like a big slab of chocolate as a gift? Here we use nuts, dried fruit, and pretzels to make reindeer faces that are set into the chocolate. The reindeer design is especially Christmassy, but you can sprinkle on any toppings you like. Just remember to use something crunchy for an interesting texture.

**Top tip:** Make smaller slabs of chocolate bark if you want to gift them to a few people!

## Method

**1** Prepare the toppings first. Put the almonds, raisins, and cranberries in separate little bowls.

**2** Break the pretzels in half for the reindeers' antlers and add to another little bowl.

**3** Line a large baking sheet with parchment paper.

**4** Break the dark chocolate into a microwavable bowl. Ask an adult to help you microwave it for 30 seconds, then stir and repeat until the chocolate is melted and smooth.

5 Ask an adult to pour the dark chocolate onto the parchment paper.

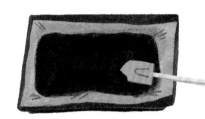

6 Use a spatula to spread it around until you have a rectangular slab of chocolate that is about the size of an 8 ½" × 11" sheet of paper.

7 Repeat step 4 with the white chocolate and leave to cool a little.

8 Drop 6 teaspoonfuls of white chocolate onto the dark chocolate slab (these will be the reindeer heads).

9 Add the pretzels for antlers, almonds for ears, raisins for eyes, and a cranberry for the nose.

10 Chill the baking sheet in the fridge and allow to set (this may take about 1 hour).

11 Once the chocolate has set, you can either give the whole slab as a present or break it into individual pieces.

12 If you are gifting this as a big slab, I suggest wrapping it in parchment paper and tying it with a ribbon. If you've broken it into pieces, use clear sandwich bags.

9

# Melting Meringue Snowpeople

Meringues are sweet and crunchy and chewy in the middle. For this recipe, your piping skills will be put to the test as we pipe meringue and then pipe chocolate on top. Decorate the snowpeople with chocolate and candies, or for a healthier option, use nuts, seeds, and dried fruit. You will need 2 piping bags for this recipe, but if you don't have any, then sandwich bags work just as well. Store the finished meringues in an airtight container to keep them from going soft.

## Ingredients

2 medium egg whites
½ cup granulated sugar
½ tsp vanilla extract
2 oz milk chocolate
54 tiny candies (or nuts, seeds, and dried fruit)

Makes 18 meringues

## Method

**1** Preheat oven to 220°F.

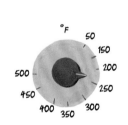

**2** Line 2 large baking sheets with parchment paper.

**3** Crack the eggs 1 at a time over a little bowl, and let the egg white drip through your fingers while containing the yolk in your open hand.

**4** Use an electric mixer to beat the egg whites until stiff and fluffy (this may take 3–5 minutes).

**5** While still whisking, add 1 teaspoonful of sugar and count to 10. Repeat until you have used up the sugar. Then add the vanilla and whisk for another 30 seconds.

**6** Rub a little of the mixture between your finger and thumb. It should be smooth, without any sugar granules.

**7** Ask a helper to hold open your piping bag, then spoon the meringue mixture inside. Bring the top of the bag together and twist.

**8** Pipe a squiggly line about 4 inches long, then add a blob for the head. Continue piping snowpeople until you've run out of mixture.

**9** Bake for 1 hour, then switch off the oven and leave the snowpeople inside the oven for another hour.

**10** Break the chocolate into a microwavable bowl. Ask an adult to help you microwave it for 30 seconds, then stir and repeat until it is melted and smooth.

**11** Ask an adult to pour the melted chocolate carefully into a smaller piping bag. (If using a sandwich bag, snip a tiny opening close to the tip.)

**12** Pipe on the eyes, mouth, and 3 blobs for buttons. Add a candy to each blob. Allow the chocolate to set before eating or gifting.

**Top tip:** Give your snowpeople some personality! You can use marshmallows and fruit leather to make hats and scarves.

# Rocky Road Squares

Are you ready to rocky-road around the Christmas tree? Then this recipe is for you! Rocky road can be made with white, milk, or dark chocolate. If you make it with white chocolate, it will look (and even have a nice crunch!) just like snow. I've suggested using graham crackers here, but you can use any cookie you like. Maybe you have some left over from other recipes in this book?

## Ingredients

13 graham cracker sheets
⅓ cup unsalted peanuts
⅔ cup dried cranberries
3 cups mini marshmallows
16 oz white chocolate
2 tsp vanilla pudding mix
⅓ cup plain yogurt
Christmas sprinkles

**Makes 16 bite-size pieces**

## Method

**1** Line an 8-inch square cake pan with parchment paper.

**2** Put the graham crackers in a sandwich bag. Bash gently with a rolling pin until crushed, then add to a mixing bowl.

**3** Add most of the peanuts and cranberries (save about ¼ to sprinkle on top), then add the marshmallows and mix everything together with a wooden spoon.

**4** Break the chocolate into pieces and add to a microwavable bowl. Ask an adult to help you microwave it for 30 seconds, then stir and repeat until it is melted and smooth.

**5** Leave the chocolate to cool a little.

**6** Add the pudding mix and yogurt to another small bowl and stir until combined.

**7** Pour the yogurt mixture into the white chocolate and stir until smooth. Add this to the mixing bowl and stir until everything is coated.

**8** Transfer to the pan and gently press down so that the mixture fills the corners of the tin and is roughly level.

**9** Top with the leftover peanuts and cranberries, then add your Christmas sprinkles.

**10** Chill the rocky road for at least 2 hours in the fridge.

**11** Once the rocky road has set, ask an adult to help you cut it into 4 rows and then each row into 4 squares so that you have 16 pieces.

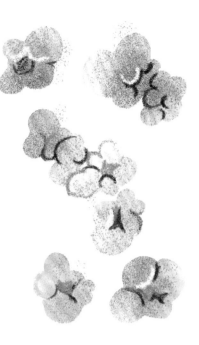

# Sweet-and-Spicy Popcorn

I love popcorn and eat it all year round. I like it sweet, but my husband likes it salty. This version is perfect for both of us as it is a little sweet *and* a little salty, and the dusting of cinnamon gives it a special Christmas twist!

**Top tip:** Package the popcorn in clear piping bags, tie the tops with ribbon, and then you have perfect gift bags!

## Ingredients

1 tsp brown sugar

¼ tsp salt

½ tsp cocoa powder

½ tsp ground cinnamon

¼ cup popcorn kernels

1 tbsp vegetable oil

2 tbsp butter

### Makes 4–6 portions

## Method

**1** Mix the sugar, salt, cocoa powder, and cinnamon together in a small bowl, then set aside.

**2** Ask an adult to help you with popping the popcorn kernels. First, measure out the popcorn kernels into a large mixing bowl.

**3** Add the oil to a medium saucepan (that has a lid) and heat on a medium setting, keeping the lid off as the oil heats up.

**4** Carefully add 2 kernels to the pan.

**5** When 1 of the kernels pops, add the butter, the rest of the kernels, and then the saucepan lid.

**6** As the popcorn pops, ask an adult to shake the pan once or twice.

**7** Once there are gaps of more than 2 seconds between pops, remove from the heat and empty the kernels into your large mixing bowl.

**8** Sprinkle on the sugar, salt, and spice mix and quickly toss together with a wooden spoon.

**9** Allow to cool before popping the popcorn in your mouth.

## Ingredients

2 cups ground almonds

⅔ cup powdered sugar

¼ cup water

½ tsp almond extract

Red food color gel

Green food color gel

**Makes 30 pieces**

# Marzipan Holly

Marzipan is my favorite thing about Christmas. I just love it SO much! Marzipan is like nutty, edible play dough, and you can use it to create whatever shapes you want. My twin brother once made me a gift of marzipan vegetables for Christmas because he only had green food coloring!

## Method

**1** Put the ground almonds and powdered sugar in a food processor and pulse twice until combined.

**2** Add the water and almond extract and pulse until the mixture looks like breadcrumbs.

**3** Tip out onto a clean surface, then squash it all together and knead until it becomes a smooth dough.

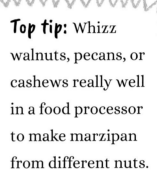

**Top tip:** Whizz walnuts, pecans, or cashews really well in a food processor to make marzipan from different nuts.

**4** Take a golf-ball-size piece of marzipan, add a small blob of red food coloring, then squish and squash the dough until it turns red.

**5** Add a blob of green food coloring to the rest of the marzipan and squish and squash it until it all turns green.

**6** Roll out the green marzipan until it is about ¼ inch thick, then cut out shapes with a holly-leaf-shaped cookie cutter. Use a dusting of powdered sugar if it is sticking to the surface.

**7** Pinch off little pieces of red marzipan and roll into small balls (for the berries).

**8** Dip your finger in water and dab the end of each holly leaf, squashing it slightly. Wait for a moment, then gently press 2 berries onto the end of each leaf.

# Marzipan Christmas Creations

If you have more food coloring and decorations, try making some different marzipan creations to share with your friends and family.

## Christmas crowns

Add a pinch of turmeric to color the marzipan a golden yellow, then use a crown cookie cutter to cut out shapes (or use a little knife to cut around a template). Decorate the crowns with nuts, seeds, dried fruit, candies, or any of your favorite toppings.

## Snowy trees

Roll green marzipan pieces into cones, snip around the sides with scissors to make branches, then dust with powdered sugar to make them look snowy.

## Marzipan potatoes

In Germany, they eat marzipan potatoes at Christmas, which are my favorite. It's fun to make potatoes—and really easy. You just roll balls of marzipan, make them a little uneven with your fingers, then dust them with cocoa powder and roll in your hands again.

## Marzipan fruits

If you're feeling creative, have a go at making traditional marzipan fruits. Use different food colorings when preparing the marzipan and see how realistic you can make your fruit.

# Party Food

## Ingredients

### Dough:

3 ¼ cups bread flour
   (plus extra for dusting)
¾ cup whole wheat flour
2 tbsp fast-acting yeast
1 tsp salt
1 ¼ cups warm water

### Sauce:

15 oz can of diced tomatoes
1 tsp dried oregano
½ tsp salt

### Toppings:

3 ½ oz cheddar cheese
3 ½ oz Monterey Jack cheese
1 red bell pepper
1 green bell pepper
8 green olives
⅓ cup canned corn
   (drained)

### Makes 6 mini pizzas

# Christmas Sweater Pizzas

Everyone loves a bright and funny Christmas sweater, and with this recipe you get to design your own AND eat it! Making pizzas is always fun, and here people can use their favorite toppings and let their imaginations run wild.

## Method

**1** In a large mixing bowl, combine the flours, yeast, salt, and water until a sticky dough forms, then allow to rest for 5 minutes.

**2** Tip the dough out onto a lightly floured surface and knead for 3 minutes (do not use any extra flour; it doesn't matter if it starts off sticky).

**3** Return the dough to the bowl, cover, and allow to rise in a warm place until it doubles in size (this will take over 1 hour).

**4** While the dough is rising, empty the diced tomatoes into a small saucepan with the oregano and salt. Simmer gently for 15 minutes, then leave to cool.

**5** Line 2 large baking sheets with parchment paper.

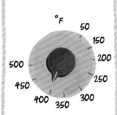

**6** Preheat oven to 400°F.

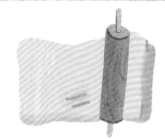

**7** On a lightly floured surface, roll out the dough until you have a rectangular shape that is about 20 × 15 inches.

**8** Using a pizza cutter, slice in half widthwise, then cut each half into 3 pieces.

**9** Cut each of those pieces into 1 big piece and 2 smaller pieces (to make the sweater body and the sleeves).

**10** Lay a big piece (for the sweater body) onto the parchment paper, then press the 2 smaller pieces (for the sleeves) onto the top corners of the sweater.

**11** Cut off ½ inch from the end of each sleeve and press these pieces onto the top of the sweater to form a neck.

**12** Repeat steps 10–11 to make the rest of your pizza sweaters, then spread on the tomato base, sprinkle on the cheese, and decorate with the rest of the toppings.

**13** Bake for 15 minutes, then allow to cool for 10 minutes before serving.

**Top tip:** Make regular round pizzas and decorate them like ornaments!

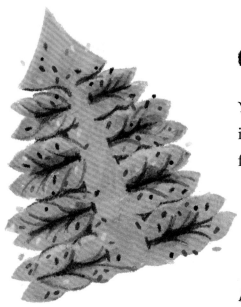

# Christmas Tree Pull-Apart Bread

You may have heard of "tear and share" bread—a big bread that is easy to pull apart into smaller pieces. This version is perfect for a party and goes well with the festive dips (p. 32).

## Ingredients

¾ cup fresh spinach

¾ cup fresh basil

¾ cup warm water

3 ½ cups bread flour (plus extra for dusting)

2 tsp fast-acting yeast

1 tsp salt

⅓ cup cheddar cheese (grated)

2 tsp milk

1 tsp maple syrup (or honey)

1 tbsp poppy seeds

1 tbsp sesame seeds

Makes 8–10 servings

## Method

**1** Line a large baking sheet with parchment paper.

**2** Put the spinach, basil, and water in a blender and blitz until you have green water.

**3** Put the flour, yeast, and salt in a mixing bowl, then add the green water and mix together to make a rough dough.

**4** Cover and leave for 3 minutes.

**5** Tip the dough out onto a lightly floured surface and knead for 5 minutes (do not use any extra flour; it doesn't matter if it starts off sticky).

**6** Return the dough to the bowl, cover, and leave in a warm place until it doubles in size (this will take at least 1 hour).

**7** On a lightly floured surface, roll out the dough to a rectangle shape that is about 14 × 10 inches.

**8** Cut away each side of the dough at an angle so that you have 1 large triangle and 2 smaller triangles.

**9** Take the 2 smaller triangles and flip them onto the baking sheet to make another large triangle shape.

**10** Sprinkle on the grated cheese, then place the remaining triangle on top.

**11** Ask an adult to help you cut 8 tabs into each side, using kitchen scissors.

**12** Gently lift each tab and twist it around a few times, then place back down.

**13** Cover and leave your tree dough to rise until it doubles in size.

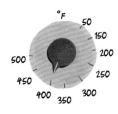

**14** Preheat oven to 400°F.

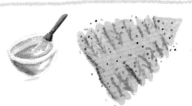

**15** Mix together the milk and maple syrup in a bowl, then brush over the tree. Sprinkle on the seeds and bake for 15 minutes, then allow to cool.

## Ingredients

½ lb Yukon Gold potatoes

⅔ cup canned corn
   (drained)

½ tsp salt

10 sheets filo pastry

2 tbsp butter

12 tsp cranberry sauce

### Makes 20 pastries

# Filo Pastry Presents

Lots of people like to give presents to each other at Christmas, and here are some tasty filo pastry presents for your Christmas party. You can make the presents personal by adding different sauce fillings for different people—I love mustard! These are best eaten warm while they're still crunchy.

## Method

**1** Peel then chop the potatoes into ½-inch cubes and add to a small saucepan with enough water to cover them.

**2** Ask an adult to help you bring the water to a boil. Simmer for 10 minutes until the potato cubes are soft, then drain.

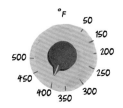

**3** Preheat oven to 400°F.

**4** Line a large baking sheet with parchment paper.

**5** In a bowl, toss together the potato cubes, corn, and salt, then set aside.

**6** Prepare the filo pastry by cutting it into squares that are about 6 × 6 inches. You need 60 squares in total (3 layers of filo per parcel).

**7** Add the butter to a small microwavable bowl and ask an adult to melt it in the microwave (about 5–10 seconds).

**8** To make the parcels, place a square of pastry on a cutting board and brush all over with a little melted butter (if you don't have a brush, use your fingers).

**9** Add another layer of pastry, brush with butter again, then add a final layer and brush with butter.

**10** Take a spoonful of filling and place in the center of the square, then add a teaspoonful of cranberry sauce on top.

**11** Gather all the sides and scrunch together at the top.

**12** Transfer to the baking sheet, then repeat steps 8–11 to make the rest of your parcels.

**13** Bake for 20 minutes until golden and crispy, then leave to cool on a cooling rack.

## Ingredients

2 ½ cups potatoes

1 ½ cups parsnips

½ tsp salt

3 oz cheddar cheese

½ cup all-purpose flour

2 medium eggs

¾ cup panko breadcrumbs

1 tsp paprika

1 tbsp vegetable oil

**Makes 14 croquettes**

# Cheesy Christmas Croquettes

Roast potatoes are often the yummiest part of a Christmas dinner, but that's because people haven't tried these cheesy Christmas croquettes yet! They are crunchy on the outside, then SO soft and creamy in the middle. You can eat them as part of a dinner or as a festive snack on their own, or simply dip them into your favorite sauce and enjoy!

## Method

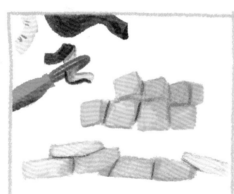

1 Peel the potatoes and parsnips and chop into ½-inch pieces.

2 Add to a saucepan with enough water to cover them. Add the salt and bring to a simmer, cooking for 10–12 minutes.

3 Ask an adult to help you drain the water. Mash until smooth, then set aside to cool.

4 Line a large baking sheet with parchment paper.

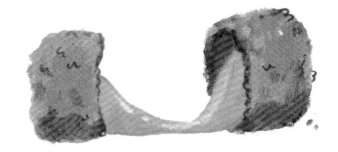

**5** Ask an adult to help you cut the cheddar into 14 cubes.

**6** Put the flour in a small bowl. Crack the eggs into another bowl and whisk with a fork.

**7** Toss together the panko breadcrumbs, paprika, and oil in another little bowl.

**8** Take a big spoonful of the mashed potato and parsnip and squash it into a disk in your hand.

  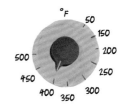

**9** Add a cube of cheese to the middle and shape the potato and parsnip around the cheese.

**10** Once all 14 are finished, pop them in the fridge for 10 minutes.

**11** Preheat oven to 400°F.

**12** Take your croquettes out of the fridge. One by one, roll them in the flour, then in the egg, then finally in the breadcrumbs. Transfer to the baking sheet.

**13** Once all the croquettes are ready, bake for 12–14 minutes until nicely golden.

**14** Allow to cool a bit before eating; otherwise the cheese will be too hot.

# Sweet-and-Sticky Sausage Rolls

I don't eat meat, so I use veggie sausages for this recipe, but you can use whatever sausages you like. The dough here needs lots of resting time in the fridge, which is the perfect moment for you to wrap your presents or decorate your Christmas tree.

## Ingredients

1 ⅛ cups bread flour
(plus extra for dusting)
1 ⅛ cups all-purpose flour
½ tsp baking powder
1 cup (2 sticks) cold
unsalted butter (diced
into ½-inch cubes)
⅔ cup cold water
12 breakfast sausages
(uncooked)
½ jar of cranberry sauce
2 tbsp milk

### Makes 24 pastries

## Method

**1** Put the flours, baking powder, and cubes of butter in a mixing bowl and toss together.

**2** Pour in the cold water, lightly mix with a spatula, then gently knead to a dough (try not to squash the butter too much; you should still be able to see whole bits of butter).

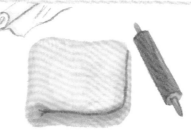

**3** On a lightly floured surface, roll out the dough until it is ½ inch thick, then fold in half, cover in plastic wrap, and chill in the fridge for 30 minutes.

**4** While the dough is chilling, ask an adult to help slice the sausages in half lengthwise and set aside (remember to wash your hands after).

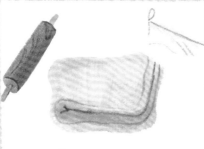

**5** Repeat step 3 one more time.

**6** Preheat oven to 350°F.

**7** Line 2 large baking sheets with parchment paper.

**8** On a lightly floured surface, roll out the pastry to make a rectangle shape, about 9 × 16 inches.

**9** Spread with the cranberry sauce, then ask an adult to help you cut the pastry widthwise into 24 equal pieces.

**10** With the sauce on the inside, wrap a pastry strip around a sausage half, then place on the baking sheet.

**11** Repeat step 10 to make all 24 wrapped sausages, then brush them all with the milk.

**12** Bake for 25 minutes until nice and golden, then leave to cool on a cooling rack.

## Ingredients

### Pastry:

6 tbsp butter (plus extra
    for greasing)

1 ⅛ cups all-purpose flour

3 tbsp whole wheat flour

¼ cup powdered sugar

1 tsp ground cinnamon

3 tbsp milk

### Filling:

½ cup strawberry jam (or
    special Christmas jam)

½ cup sliced almonds

2 tbsp dried cranberries

¼ cup raisins

1 tbsp powdered sugar (for
    dusting)

Makes 12 pies

# Fruity "Mince" Pies

When you smell a mince pie, you know it's Christmas. These mince pies are especially for kids as they are fruity like a Christmas jam tart. They fill the kitchen with lovely smells when they are baking because of the cinnamon in the pastry. I used circular and star-shaped cutters for this recipe, but you can try out all kinds of shapes to top the pies.

## Method

**1** Add the butter, flours, powdered sugar, and cinnamon to a food processor and whizz until you have breadcrumbs. Add the milk and whizz again. (If you don't have a food processor, simply rub the butter into the dry ingredients, then stir in the milk with a blunt knife.)

**2** Tip out onto a clean surface and bring together with your hands, squashing it until you have a dough.

**3** Wrap and chill in the fridge for 30 minutes.

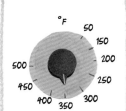 **4** Preheat oven to 350°F.

 **5** To make the filling, mix together the jam, almonds, cranberries, and raisins.

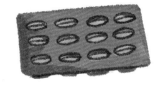 **6** Grease a 12-hole cupcake tin with butter, then take the pastry out of the fridge and roll it out on a lightly floured surface until it is ¼ inch thick.

 **7** Use a 4-inch cookie cutter to cut 12 disks out of the pastry.

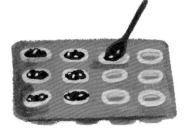 **8** Press each pastry disk into a hole in the tin and add a big spoonful of the filling to each pastry case.

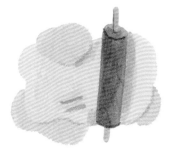 **9** Bring all the leftover pastry together and roll out again.

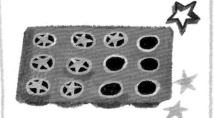 **10** Use a star-shaped cutter to cut out 12 stars, then place a star on top of each pie.

 **11** Bake for 25 minutes, then leave to cool on a cooling rack. Dust with powdered sugar before serving.

# Festive Dips

Red and green are the most Christmassy colors EVER. Since there are loads of red and green vegetables, this means making Christmas dips is easy! The whizzed-up cannellini beans make these dips super smooth and all the more delicious. Serve your dips with some carrot or cucumber sticks or even the Christmas Tree Pull-Apart Bread (p. 22).

## Ingredients

### Red dip:

⅓ cup roasted red peppers from a jar (drained)

½ cup cannellini beans (drained)

1 garlic clove (minced)

¼ cup walnuts

A pinch of salt

1 tsp ground cumin

### Green dip:

1 ripe avocado

½ cup cannellini beans (drained)

A pinch of salt

¾ cup fresh basil

1 garlic clove (minced)

### Makes 2 big bowls of dip

## Method

**1** For the red dip, add the red peppers and cannellini beans to a food processor, then whizz together. If you want the dip to be very smooth, keep whizzing for another 2 minutes. (Use the remaining beans for your green dip.)

**2** Add the garlic, walnuts, salt, and cumin, then whizz everything together until combined. Scoop the dip into a small bowl, ready to serve. Ask an adult to help you clean the food processor before you make the green dip.

**3** For the green dip, ask an adult to help you slice the avocado in half, remove the pit, and scoop out the flesh with a spoon.

**4** Add the avocado, cannellini beans, salt, basil, and garlic to the food processor and whizz until smooth.

**5** Serve with vegetable sticks, breadsticks, or crackers, and enjoy!

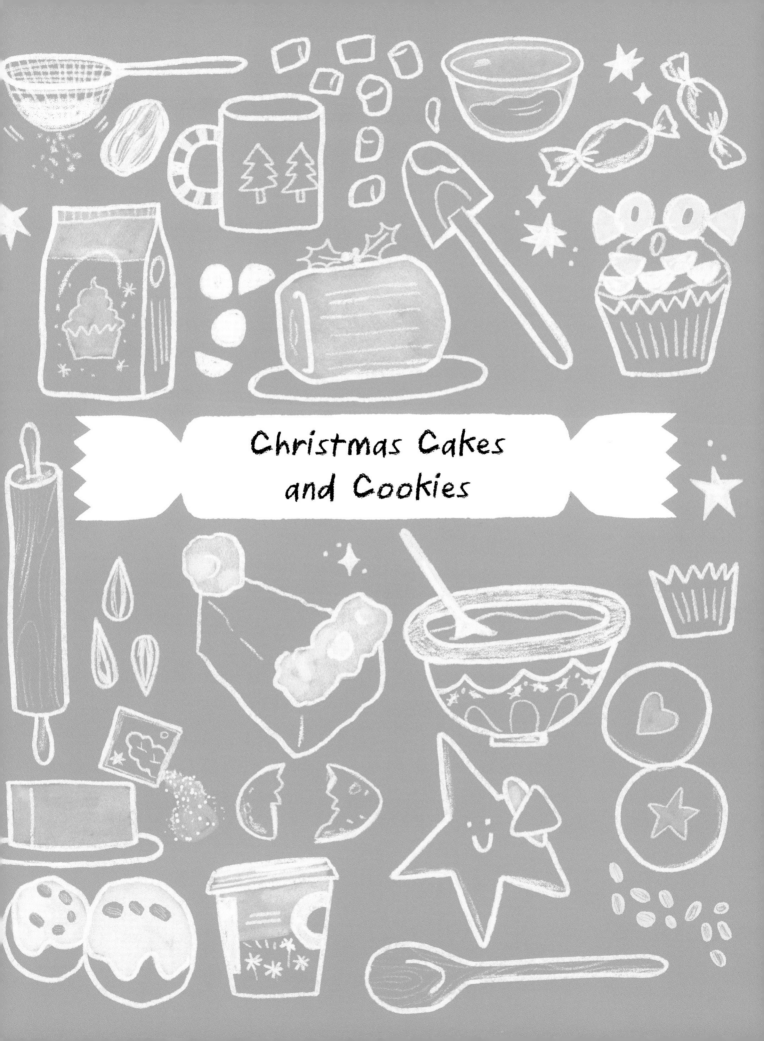

# Christmas Cakes and Cookies

## Ingredients

### Cupcakes:

2/3 cup granulated sugar

½ cup vegetable oil

2 medium eggs

1 tsp vanilla extract

¾ cup grated russet potato

1 cup all-purpose flour

1 ½ tsp baking powder

¼ cup raisins

### Decoration:

2 tbsp unsalted butter (at
    room temperature)

¾ cup powdered sugar

1 tsp vanilla extract

Hot water (boiled)

80 white chocolate buttons

36 raisins

Makes 12 cupcakes

# Snowy Owl Cupcakes

Owls are so cute, so who wouldn't want an owl cupcake? Snowy owls are all white and live in snowy areas of the world. They are hard to see because they are camouflaged in the snow. These cupcakes can't hide as easily—they're so delicious everyone will seek them out.

# Method

**1** Preheat oven to 300°F.

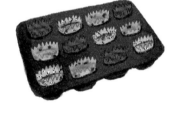

**2** Prepare a 12-hole cupcake tin with cupcake liners.

**3** Beat together the sugar, oil, eggs, and vanilla.

**4** Peel the potatoes, then finely grate. Add to the mixture and stir together.

**5** Fold in the flour and baking powder until combined, then add the raisins and do a final mix.

**6** Divide the mixture equally between the cupcake liners (about ¾ full) and bake for 18 minutes.

**7** Allow to cool fully before decorating.

**8** Mix together the butter, powdered sugar, and vanilla (it will look very crumbly, but don't worry).

**9** Beat in a teaspoonful of boiling water. Keep adding teaspoonfuls of boiling water until you have a thick icing.

**10** Spread a thin layer of icing onto each cupcake.

**11** Carefully cut some chocolate buttons in half, then layer them over the bottom half of the icing to make the feathers.

**12** Add whole chocolate buttons for the eyes and pieces for the tufts. Using a little of the leftover icing, stick raisins in place for a beak and pupils.

**Top tip:** Add 2 teaspoonfuls of cocoa powder to the icing and use milk chocolate buttons to make tawny owls.

# Red Velvet Santa Hats

These cakes are quick and easy to make and taste delicious! Red velvet cake is actually a chocolate cake, but you don't use a lot of cocoa powder, so the cake doesn't come out brown. It is up to you how much red food coloring you put into the cake. The yogurt in the batter helps the cake rise and makes it really soft.

## Ingredients

### Cakes:

⅓ cup vegetable oil (plus extra for greasing)

¾ cup granulated sugar

⅓ cup plain yogurt

1 tsp vanilla extract

Red food color gel

1 medium egg

1 cup all-purpose flour

1 tsp cocoa powder

½ tsp baking powder

½ tsp baking soda

### Decoration:

¼ cup powdered sugar

1 cup mini marshmallows

Makes 8 cakes

## Method

**1** Preheat oven to 300°F.

**2** Grease the inside of an 8-inch round cake pan with a little oil, making sure you cover all of the pan.

**3** In a large mixing bowl, beat together the oil, sugar, yogurt, vanilla, and red food coloring.

**4** Crack the egg over the bowl and beat into the mixture.

5 In a separate bowl, toss together the flour, cocoa powder, baking powder, and baking soda.

6 Tip the dry ingredients into the wet mixture and stir until combined.

7 Pour into the pan and bake for 25–30 minutes (or until a skewer comes out clean).

8 Ask an adult to take the pan out of the oven, then let the cake cool on a cooling rack before removing it from the pan.

9 Slice the cake in half, then in half again and again until you have 8 slices.

10 Pour the powdered sugar into a bowl, then add 2 teaspoonfuls of water and mix.

11 Mix together and keep adding a teaspoonful of water until your icing becomes thick and sticky.

12 Cut the marshmallows into small pieces (about ¼ inch) on a cutting board, then add to the icing.

13 Spoon the marshmallow icing onto the rims and tops of the cake slices so that they look like Santa hats!

## Ingredients

### Cake:

⅔ cup granulated sugar

⅔ cup packed brown sugar

1 cup vegetable oil

4 medium eggs

2 cups grated carrots

2 cups all-purpose flour

3 tsp baking powder

1 tsp ground cinnamon

### Decoration:

⅔ cup powdered sugar

½ tsp almond extract

2 tbsp water

Christmas sprinkles

4 strawberry licorice laces

Makes 12 servings

# Christmas Cracker Cake

I LOVE carrot cake, but you can also use parsnip, sweet potato, or butternut squash instead in this recipe. Did you know that root vegetables were popular ingredients in baking when we didn't have a lot of sugar or butter? They make cakes soft and sweet as well as a little bit healthier, so everyone's happy!

## Method

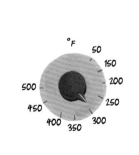

**1** Preheat oven to 300°F.

**2** Grease and line two 8 ½-inch loaf pans with parchment paper.

**3** In a large mixing bowl, beat together the sugars and oil until smooth. Crack the eggs, one at a time, over the bowl, then beat into the mixture.

**4** Ask an adult to help you peel and finely grate the carrots. Add to the bowl and mix into the batter.

**5** Add the flour, baking powder, and cinnamon and stir until just combined.

**6** Divide the mixture between the 2 pans and bake for 30–40 minutes (or until a skewer comes out clean). For the first 20 minutes, try not to open the oven, to prevent the cakes from collapsing.

**7** Allow to cool completely, then turn the cakes out of the pans and peel off the parchment paper.

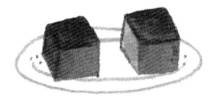

**8** Turn each cake upside down. Place 1 in the middle of a plate, then cut the other in half so that you have 2 square pieces.

**9** Remove triangles of cake from 1 side of each cake half, then place each half at either end of the second cake.

**10** Beat together the powdered sugar, almond extract, and water until you have a thick icing.

**11** Spread the icing onto the cake and add your sprinkles.

**12** Tie the licorice laces into bows and stick one at each end to make ribbons.

# Mini Chocolate Logs

*Bûche de Noël*, or Yule log, is a traditional chocolate Christmas cake originally from France and is now baked at Christmastime in lots of countries. It's a light, decadent cake that is filled with buttercream and rolled up to make a log shape. Don't worry if your sponge cracks a little as you wrap it up. The cake will still taste delicious and be VERY chocolatey, which is the most important thing.

## Ingredients

### Cakes:

3 medium eggs

½ cup granulated sugar

⅔ cup all-purpose flour

¼ cup cocoa powder

½ tsp baking powder

### Decoration:

2 tbsp butter (plus extra
    for greasing)

⅓ cup powdered sugar

1 tsp vanilla extract

A little hot water (boiled)

8 oz dark chocolate

Makes 8 logs

## Method

**1** Preheat oven to 350°F.

**2** Grease the inside of a 9 × 13 inch jelly roll pan with butter and line it with parchment paper.

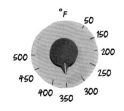

**3** Crack the eggs into a large mixing bowl, then add the sugar. Use an electric mixer to beat them together until you have a thick mixture that leaves a trail like a ribbon.

**4** Toss together the flour, cocoa powder, and baking powder in another bowl, then add to the egg mixture, a bit at a time, gently folding it in with a spatula to keep it light and airy.

**5** Pour the mixture carefully into the pan and use a spatula to spread it out, then bake for 15 minutes.

6 Allow to cool for 2 minutes, then turn out onto a cooling rack, keeping the parchment paper in place.

7 While the cake is still warm, roll up 1 short side until you reach the middle. Then roll the other side to the middle, wrap in a tea towel, and leave to cool.

8 To make the buttercream, rub the butter and powdered sugar together until you have a crumbly mixture. Add the vanilla and 1 teaspoonful of hot water, then beat until smooth (add another teaspoonful of hot water if you need to).

9 Unwrap your cake and cut down the middle so you have 2 rolls.

10 Unroll each cake and remove the parchment paper. Spread each cake with a thin layer of buttercream, then roll up again tightly, using your tea towel.

11 Slice each roll into 4 so that you have 8 mini rolls.

12 Ask an adult to help you microwave the chocolate for 30 seconds, then stir and repeat until it is melted and smooth.

13 Allow the chocolate to cool down a little, then spoon it over the rolls and spread it around. Use a fork to make marks along the rolls so that they look like little logs.

14 Allow the chocolate logs to set in the fridge for at least 10 minutes, then serve.

# Snowpeople Scones

Not everyone gets snow at Christmastime, but everyone can build a scone snowperson. The recipe here gives you the basic decoration, but you can use candies, seeds, nuts, fruits, or whatever you can think of to add more personality to your snowpeople.

## Ingredients

### Scones:
2 ¾ cups all-purpose flour
  (plus extra for dusting)
2 tsp baking powder
¼ cup granulated sugar
6 tbsp unsalted butter
⅔ cup milk
1 tsp vanilla extract
1 tsp lemon juice

### Decoration:
¾ cup powdered sugar
2 tbsp water
1 tsp vanilla extract
A handful of raisins

Makes 8
scones

## Method

*1* Preheat oven to 350°F.

*2* Line a large baking sheet with parchment paper.

*3* In a mixing bowl, rub the flour, baking powder, sugar, and butter together with your fingers until it looks like breadcrumbs (or whizz in a food processor).

*4* Stir together the milk, vanilla, and lemon in a measuring cup, then pour into the mixing bowl.

5 Mix until you have a dough, then leave to sit for 5 minutes.

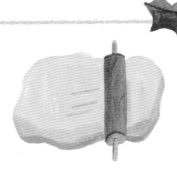

6 On a lightly floured surface, roll out the dough until it is ½ inch thick.

7 Cut out 4 scones using a 1 ½-inch cookie cutter and 4 scones using a 2-inch cookie cutter, then transfer to the baking sheet.

8 Bake for 15 minutes, until just golden, then allow to cool on a cooling rack.

9 Beat together the powdered sugar, water, and vanilla until you have a thick icing.

10 Dip the top of a smaller scone into the icing, then dip a larger scone. Place them next to each other to make a snowperson.

11 Add raisins for the eyes, mouth, and buttons to finish.

12 Repeat steps 10 and 11 to make the rest of your snowpeople, transfer to plates, then serve.

**Top tip:** If you don't have cookie cutters, shape the dough with your hands.

## Ingredients

1 ¾ cups all-purpose flour
(plus extra for dusting)
1 tbsp cocoa powder
½ tsp ground cinnamon
A pinch of salt
⅓ cup packed brown sugar
½ cup (1 stick) unsalted
butter (cold)
¼ cup milk
20 hard candies

Makes 30 cookies

## Method

# Stained-Glass Cookies

These cookies look so pretty, especially if you hold them up to the light. For this recipe, I've suggested using a circular cookie cutter as well as a heart-shaped cutter for the centers, but you can use whatever shapes you like. These cookies are a great present to give to your best friend. Just wrap a few up in a little parchment paper, tie with a ribbon, and add a gift tag. Lovely!

**1** Line 2 baking sheets with parchment paper.

**2** In a mixing bowl, toss together the flour, cocoa powder, cinnamon, salt, and sugar. Cut the cold butter into small cubes and add to the mixing bowl.

**3** Rub together with your fingers until the mixture looks like breadcrumbs.

**4** Add the milk, a bit at a time, then squish the mixture until it becomes a dough.

**5** Wrap and chill in the fridge for 30 minutes.

**6** Unwrap all the hard candies of one color and add to a sandwich bag. Ask an adult to help you crush the candies into crumbs using a hammer (don't use a wooden rolling pin or board as they could dent).

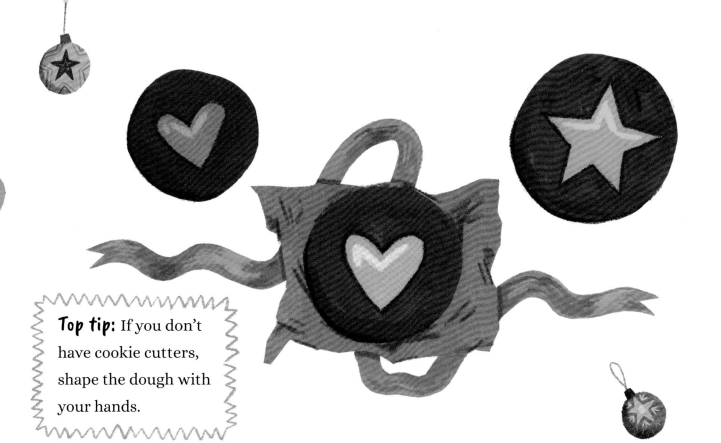

**Top tip:** If you don't have cookie cutters, shape the dough with your hands.

**7** Repeat step 6 for different colors in separate bags and set them aside in small bowls.

**8** On a lightly floured surface, roll out the dough until it is ¼ inch thick.

**9** Cut out disks using a 3-inch cookie cutter, then cut out the centers using a heart-shaped cutter.

**10** Add to the baking sheets and transfer to the fridge to chill for 20 minutes.

**11** Preheat oven to 350°F.

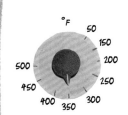

**12** Take the trays out of the fridge and sprinkle the candy crumbs into the center of each cookie.

**13** Bake for 10–12 minutes. Allow to cool completely before removing from the baking sheets.

45

## Ingredients

### Cookies:

⅔ cup rolled oats

1 cup all-purpose flour (plus extra for dusting)

⅓ cup whole wheat flour

½ tsp allspice

A pinch of salt

6 tbsp unsalted butter

2 tbsp smooth peanut butter

⅓ cup packed brown sugar

2 tbsp honey

1 medium egg

### Decoration:

1 tbsp cocoa powder

1 tbsp sunflower seeds

1 tbsp poppy seeds

1 tbsp sliced almonds

1 tbsp coconut flakes

A handful of raisins

6 maraschino cherries

**Makes 30 cookies**

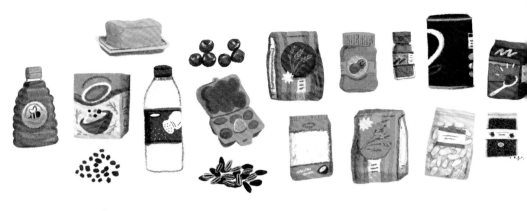

# Family-Favorite Cookies

Christmas is a time for families to get together. I love making these cookies that look like my family, and I include all my cousins, aunties, and uncles too. I also include my pets! The best part is watching my family try to guess which cookie belongs to each person.

## Method

1 Line 2 large baking sheets with parchment paper.

2 Put the oats in a food processor and blitz until you have a fine powder.

3 Add the flours, allspice, salt, butter, and peanut butter and blitz until combined.

4 Add the sugar and honey. Crack the egg into the food processor, then pulse everything together until you have a dough.

**5** Tip out onto a lightly floured surface and bring together in a ball.

**6** Wrap and chill the dough in the fridge for 1 hour.

**7** Add your decorations to little bowls. Ask an adult to help you slice the cherries into small strips.

**8** Take a big teaspoonful of dough, roll in floured hands, and press into a face shape.

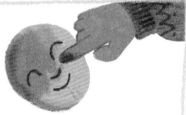

**9** Dip your finger in the cocoa powder and pad all over the face until it looks close to your family member's skin tone.

**10** Dip your fingers in water and dab the water along the hairline, then stick on seeds for hair.

**11** Press on seeds, nuts, or dried fruit to make eyes and noses. You can also use the edge of a spoon to create a smiley mouth, or take blobs of dough to make other facial features.

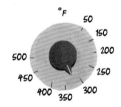

**12** Preheat oven to 325°F.

**13** Transfer the cookies to the baking sheets and chill in the fridge for 30 minutes.

**14** Bake for 15 minutes, then allow to cool for a few minutes before transferring to a cooling rack to cool fully.

# Christmas Reindeer Cookies

These cookies are clever because you don't need a reindeer cookie cutter to make them. Instead, we use a small gingerbread-person cutter and just turn the shape upside down so that it looks like a reindeer's face. Cool, right?

## Method

**1** Line 2 large baking sheets with parchment paper.

**2** Put the butter and dates in a food processor and blitz until smooth.

**3** Add the powdered sugar, cocoa powder, and ginger and whizz again.

**4** Add the flour and pulse a couple of times until combined.

**5** Add 2 teaspoonfuls of cold water to soften the mixture and pulse again, then tip out onto a surface. Gather up the mixture with your hands until you have a smooth ball of dough.

**6** Wrap and chill in the fridge for 30 minutes.

## Ingredients

5 tbsp unsalted butter

5 soft pitted dates

¼ cup powdered sugar

1 tbsp cocoa powder

½ tsp ground ginger

1 cup all-purpose flour
(plus extra for dusting)

2 tsp cold water

3 ½ oz white chocolate

24 raisins

24 mini pretzels
(broken into halves)

Makes 24 cookies

 **7** On a lightly floured surface, roll out the dough until it is ¼ inch thick.

 **8** Cut out cookies using a gingerbread-person cutter, no bigger than 4 inches tall, and transfer to the baking sheets.

 **9** Chill in the fridge for another 30 minutes.

 **10** Preheat oven to 300°F.

 **11** Bake for 14 minutes, then allow to cool completely on a cooling rack.

 **12** Break the chocolate into pieces and add to a microwavable bowl. Ask an adult to help you microwave it for 30 seconds, then stir and repeat until it is melted and smooth.

 **13** Ask an adult to carefully transfer the chocolate to a small piping bag.

 **14** Pipe blobs of chocolate for the eyes and nose, then place a raisin onto the nose blob.

 **15** Pipe on ears, then add 2 blobs to the middle of the cookie. Stick the pretzel antlers onto the blobs, then leave your cookies to set.

## Ingredients

5 tbsp unsalted butter

¼ granulated sugar

¾ cup all-purpose flour
(plus extra for dusting)

¼ cup whole wheat flour

1 tsp ground cinnamon

1 tsp cocoa powder

1 egg

24 almonds

Makes 24
cookies

# Gifting Cookies

Sometimes bakes can be cute, and these cookies are the cutest! This recipe uses almonds, but you can make the cookies hold on to whichever type of nut you like. A couple of minutes more or less can make a difference to your cookies—if you overbake them, they'll be crunchier, and if you underbake them, they'll be soft. Experiment to find your ideal texture and have fun!

**Top tip:** Make a hole in the top point of the cookie before baking and then hang the baked star on your Christmas tree.

## Method

*1* Line a large baking sheet with parchment paper.

*2* Ask an adult to melt the butter and sugar together in a small saucepan over a low heat.

*3* Toss together the flours, cinnamon, and cocoa powder in a mixing bowl.

**4** Ask an adult to help you pour in the butter mixture and stir until combined.

**5** Crack the egg into the bowl and beat until the batter is thoroughly combined and shiny (don't worry if it looks very wet at this stage).

**6** Lay a piece of plastic wrap in another mixing bowl, then pour the cookie mixture into the middle. Bring the plastic wrap together and twist, then chill the bowl in the fridge for 1 hour.

**7** On a lightly floured surface, tip out the dough and roll it out until it is about ¼ inch thick.

**8** Cut out stars from the dough using a 3-inch star-shaped cookie cutter. Bring the extra dough together, re-roll, and cut out stars until you have 24 cookies.

**9** Place an almond on 1 of the star points on each cookie, then fold over the point.

**10** Add eyes using a skewer and make a mouth using the edge of a teaspoon, then carefully place the cookies on the lined baking sheet. Chill the sheet in the fridge for 30 minutes.

**11** Preheat oven to 325°F.

**12** Once the cookies have chilled, bake them for 12–14 minutes until golden. Allow to cool before serving on a pretty plate.

## Ingredients

½ cup rolled oats

⅔ cup milk

1 cup (2 sticks) unsalted
  butter

⅔ cup granulated sugar

1 tsp vanilla extract

2 ⅓ cups all-purpose flour

2 tsp cornstarch

A pinch of salt

½ jar of Christmas jam
  (or strawberry jam)

**Makes 20 cookies**

# Christmas Thumbprint Cookies

I love eating oatmeal for breakfast, and one time I made too much, so I decided to turn the leftover oatmeal into cookies! Oats make the cookies really soft, and the jam makes them extra delicious. You can use your special Christmas jam (p. 2), or any leftover strawberry or raspberry jam. Whatever you choose, these soft and crumbly cookies will taste yummy.

## Method

**1** Line a large baking sheet with parchment paper.

**2** Add the oats and milk to a small saucepan and gently heat for about 3 minutes, stirring until thick. Alternatively, cook the milk and oats in the microwave for 1 minute.

**3** Next, add the oats, butter, sugar, vanilla, flour, cornstarch, and salt to a food processor. Whizz until the mixture starts coming together as a dough.

**4** The mixture will be very soft, so take big spoonfuls of mixture and blob them onto the baking sheet, keeping the cookies at least an inch apart.

**5** Put the sheet in the freezer for 30 minutes.

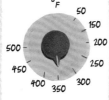

**6** Preheat oven to 350°F.

**7** Remove the sheet from the freezer, then push your thumb into the middle of each cookie. Fill each thumbprint shape with a teaspoonful of jam.

**8** Bake for 20 minutes, or until the cookies just start to turn golden brown. Allow to cool on a cooling rack (the jam will be very hot), then serve.

# Festive Showstoppers

## Ingredients

### Bread:

3 ¾ cups bread flour (plus extra for dusting)

¼ tsp ground turmeric

2 tsp fast-acting yeast

1 tsp fine salt

1 ¼ cups warm water

Zest of 1 orange

⅓ cup raisins

¼ cup currants

¼ cup candied orange peel

1 medium egg

### Decoration:

Juice of 1 orange

⅔ cup powdered sugar

10–12 maraschino cherries

¼ cup sliced almonds

Christmas sprinkles

### Makes 12 servings

# Golden Crown Bread

The paper crowns you get in Christmas crackers are so fun to wear. For this recipe, we make a sweet and doughy bread that is shaped like a crown. It is based on a Portuguese Christmas cake called a *bolo-rei*, which is a sweet bread that turns beautifully golden when baked. It's the perfect treat to share at this special time of year.

## Method

**1** Line a large baking sheet with parchment paper.

**2** In a mixing bowl, toss together the flour, turmeric, yeast, and salt.

**3** Zest the orange and add to a cup of warm water. (Set the orange aside for step 14.)

**4** Pour the zesty liquid into the mixing bowl and stir until a sticky dough forms.

**5** Sprinkle with the dried fruit and candied orange peel, then cover and let rest for 5 minutes.

 **6** Knead the bread in the mixing bowl for 5 minutes (do not add extra flour; it doesn't matter if it is a little sticky).

 **7** Cover and leave to rise in a warm place until it doubles in size (this will take at least 1 hour).

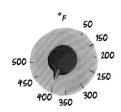 **8** On a lightly floured surface, shape the dough into a ball. Push your fingers through the middle, then stretch the bread out until the hole in the middle is about 8 inches wide.

 **9** Place on the baking sheet, cover, and leave to rise until it doubles in size.

 **10** Preheat oven to 400°F.

 **11** Whisk the egg in a bowl with a fork, then brush the egg onto the bread.

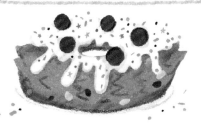 **12** Use scissors to make big snips all over the top of the bread.

 **13** Bake for 25 minutes, then leave to cool on a cooling rack.

 **14** Squeeze the orange into a bowl and mix 2 tablespoons of the juice with the powdered sugar.

**15** Dollop the icing onto the cooled bread, then dot with the cherries, nuts, and your Christmas sprinkles.

## Ingredients

20 graham cracker sheets

2 cups mini marshmallows

½ cup dried cranberries

½ cup raisins

16 oz chocolate
   (milk or dark)

½ cup light corn syrup

½ cup (1 stick) unsalted
   butter

3 ½ oz white chocolate

Makes 12 servings

## Method

# Chocolate Christmas Pudding

Christmas pudding is one of the most famous Christmas desserts EVER, but lots of people don't like eating it! I have never met anyone who doesn't like rocky road, however. The answer is simple: make a rocky road that looks like a Christmas pudding!

**1** Line a small glass bowl (about 8 inches wide) with plastic wrap.

**2** Put the graham crackers in a sandwich bag and gently bash with a rolling pin. You want to break the crackers into chunks, not into powder, so don't bash them too hard! Add the chunks to a large mixing bowl.

**3** Chop the marshmallows into little cubes and add to the bowl along with the cranberries and raisins.

**4** Break the chocolate into pieces and add to a measuring or mixing cup.

**5** Ask an adult to help you gently heat the syrup and butter in a saucepan over a low heat, stirring continuously until the butter is melted.

**6** Pour the sticky butter mixture over the chocolate and whizz with an immersion blender until smooth.

**7** Add the chocolate mixture to the mixing bowl and stir until combined.

**8** Spoon the rocky road mixture into the lined bowl, then chill it in the fridge for 2 hours.

**9** When the chocolate has set, tip the bowl upside down and peel away the plastic wrap.

**10** Break the white chocolate into a microwavable bowl. Ask an adult to help you microwave it for 30 seconds, then stir and repeat until it is melted and smooth.

**11** Leave to cool for 10 minutes, then ask an adult to help pour the white chocolate carefully over the pudding and top with a clean sprig of holly.

**12** Chill your chocolatey pudding in the fridge until everyone is ready to eat it, then ask an adult to carve slices.

## Ingredients

**Gingerbread:**

1 cup (2 sticks) unsalted butter

1 cup packed brown sugar

⅓ cup honey

4 ⅔ cups all-purpose flour

1 tsp baking soda

3 tsp ground ginger

½ tsp ground cinnamon

1 medium egg

**Decoration:**

2 cups powdered sugar

Sliced almonds

Pumpkin seeds

Raisins, currants, dried cranberries

Small candies

Chocolate buttons

**Makes 8 small gingerbread houses**

# Mini Gingerbread Village

Making a gingerbread house is fun, and the result looks amazing, but sticking the house parts together can be fiddly. Keep going with it and you'll soon have an entire gingerbread village! The key here is to make sure your icing is thick enough to form a good cement. For this recipe, you'll need a piping bag fitted with a nozzle so you can pipe decorations around the outsides of the houses.

## Method

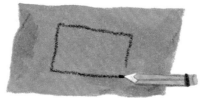

**1** Draw a rectangle (about 4 × 3 inches) and a triangle (2 ½ inches across and 3 inches tall) on a piece of parchment paper, then cut them out. These will be your templates for your gingerbread houses.

**2** Line 2–4 large baking sheets with parchment paper.

**3** In a saucepan, gently melt the butter, sugar, and honey over a low heat. Remove from the heat and add the flour, baking soda, and spices.

**4** Crack the egg over a bowl and let the egg white drip through your fingers, while containing the yolk in your open hand.

**5** Add the yolk to the saucepan and mix the ingredients together until it forms a dough. Keep the egg white for the icing.

**6** Lay a large piece of parchment paper on a work surface, then tip half of the dough onto it. Lay another piece on top, then roll the dough out until it is ¼ inch thick.

**7** Remove the top layer of parchment paper, then place your rectangle and triangle templates gently on the dough.

**8** Use a blunt knife to carefully cut around the templates so that you have 16 triangles and 16 rectangles.

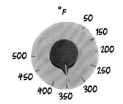

**9** Preheat oven to 350°F.

**10** Put the baking sheets in the fridge until the oven is up to temperature.

**11** Bake the cookies for 12–14 minutes, until they are just browning at the edges, then allow to cool fully on the trays.

**12** Whisk together the egg white with the powdered sugar until you have a smooth, thick icing, then transfer to the piping bag (if too thick, add a teaspoonful of water until ketchup consistency).

**13** To make a house, pipe icing along the side edges of 2 triangles and then attach a rectangle on each side. Let the icing set until it goes really hard (this will take at least 2 hours).

**14** Once the houses are stuck together, use the remaining icing to pipe on your decorations, sticking on the nuts, seeds, dried fruit, candies, and chocolate.

**David Atherton** is the 2019 winner of *The Great British Baking Show*. David's cookbooks for children—*Bake, Make, and Learn to Cook*; *Bake, Make, and Learn to Cook Vegetarian*; and *David Atherton's Baking Book for Kids*—have inspired a generation of children to create healthy, imaginative recipes for their friends and family. David is a food writer and an international health adviser for a charity. He has worked on health programs around the world and never misses an opportunity to explore a new food culture. David is passionate about ensuring that children grow up as food lovers and understand how to make tasty, healthy food.

**Katie Cottle** is a Welsh illustrator who now lives in England. Katie has illustrated a number of children's books, and she's written a few too. Katie uses lots of bright colors (orange being a particular favorite), uses lots of texture, and has lots of fun with characters. When she's not drawing, she's probably daydreaming about her future pets or feeding the ducks that live nearby.